Karl Marx

Nigel Hunter

Illustrations by Chris Higham

The Bookwright Press
New York · 1987

Great Lives

Beethoven
Louis Braille
Captain Cook
Marie Curie
Einstein
Queen Elizabeth I
Queen Elizabeth II
Anne Frank
Gandhi
Helen Keller

John F. Kennedy
Martin Luther King, Jr.
John Lennon
Ferdinand Magellan
Karl Marx
Napoleon
Florence Nightingale
Elvis Presley
William Shakespeare
Mother Teresa

First published in 1987 by
Wayland (Publishers) Limited
61 Western Road, Hove
East Sussex BN3 1JD, England

© Copyright 1987 Wayland (Publishers) Limited

First published in the
United States in 1987 by
The Bookwright Press
387 Park Avenue South
New York, NY 10016

ISBN 0–531–18133–2

Library of Congress Catalog Card Number: 86–73117

Phototypeset by Kalligraphics Ltd, Redhill, Surrey
Printed in Italy by G. Canale & C.S.p.A., Turin

Contents

A man who changed the world

In late middle age, Karl Marx liked nothing better than to chase around the garden with a grandchild perched on his shoulders, and two of his closest friends hitched up as "horses" in front. He looked fairly harmless. His neighbors might have been surprised to learn that he and his friends were on police files throughout Europe as dangerous revolutionaries. They would certainly have been astonished to know that a hundred years later, a third of the world's nations would revere Marx and one of his friends, Friedrich Engels, as the founding fathers of their systems of government.

Marx had always seemed quite an ordinary kind of man. When his daughters were small, the family often walked from their home in central London to Hampstead Heath, for a Sunday picnic. Sometimes it was a

Marx the family man in a playful mood with friends.

As a revolutionary writer Marx sought to change the world.

sizeable party, with several friends and guests invited. While the girls played, the adults talked politics, discussing the events of the week and considering various solutions to the world's great problems. Returning home, they sang popular ballads and folk songs, and Marx entertained them all with long passages from Shakespeare, and German and Italian poems that he knew by heart.

The Marx family were never wealthy; and sometimes they were so poor that, as Marx himself once said, "everything that was not nailed down" had to go to the pawnshop. Marx spent most of his life reading and writing. Through his writings, he aimed to overcome – for all humanity, for all time – all the conditions that led to extremes of wealth and poverty. His own personal life was a great struggle. But his main concern was the "greater struggle" of humankind to free itself from the bonds of misery. Nowadays, "Marxists" and "anti-Marxists" divide the world. Whatever some of us might prefer, Karl Marx's lifework cannot be wished away.

Beginnings

Karl Marx was born in a small German town called Trier, on May 5, 1818. He came from a Jewish background. Many of his forebears had been rabbis – teachers, scholars and leaders of the Jewish community, but his father, Heinrich, had recently converted to Christianity. He had done this partly for religious reasons, but also because, in Germany in those days, laws against Jews made it hard for them to do well in their professions. Having thus safeguarded his career, Heinrich Marx went on to become a well-respected lawyer.

Karl's mother, Henrietta, was entirely devoted to the care of her family. Altogether, she bore eight children, but most, to her great distress, died young. Karl was her second child, and his father's favorite. Very little is known of Karl's early childhood. The record begins with his entrance into the local high school in 1830, when he was twelve years old.

As a schoolboy Karl was interested in social issues.

Karl was a fairly average school student, obtaining his best results in German, history and the classics (Greek and Latin). But it was during his school years that he first became interested in social issues. Some of his teachers were politically much more liberal than most people in Germany at that time. His headmaster, who taught him history, and who was eventually dismissed because of his progressive, democratic opinions, influenced him deeply. In his last

Karl was considered to be a fine-looking young man.

The house where Karl Marx lived in the German town of Trier. He was born in 1818.

school essay, "On the Choice of a Profession," the young Karl Marx was already very sure of his own future goals: "According to History, the greatest men are those who have worked for the general good. Experience calls him the happiest who has made most people happy," he wrote. This was a lofty ambition, and a difficult one to live up to. But Karl was a very determined young man.

7

Conflict and progress

At the age of seventeen, Marx became a student at Bonn University. His father wanted him to study law, but his real interests lay elsewhere. He spent much of his time reading the classical mythology of Ancient Greece and Rome, and studying the history of art. He also wrote poetry with great enthusiasm, producing vast amounts of Romantic-style verse. He became deeply involved with the boistrous social life of his fellow students, drinking, brawling – once even, fighting a duel – and going heavily into debt. His father was torn between admiration for his son's intelligence and exasperation at his willfulness, and what seemed a waste of his talents. Antagonism between them ended only with

Karl was sometimes involved in brawls as a student.

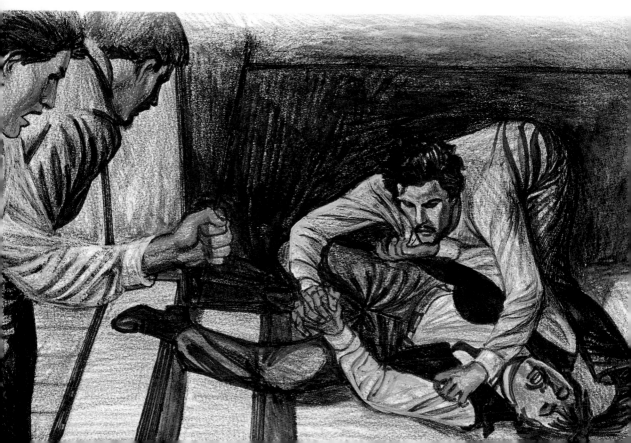

Heinrich's death, in 1838.

After a year in Bonn, Marx transferred to the University of Berlin. Meanwhile, he had become secretly engaged to Jenny von Westphalen, whom he had known since childhood. Jenny's father, a Prussian aristocrat, had first aroused Marx's interest in literature some years earlier and from now on, he dedicated most of his poetry to her.

In Berlin, although he was still supposed to be studying law, Marx became more and more interested in two other subjects: history and philosophy.

At Berlin University, Karl began to study seriously.

Jenny von Westphalen and Karl became engaged secretly.

Philosophy dealt with all the deepest, most difficult questions of life. It covered the whole field of human thought and behavior through the ages. Marx worked hard during these years, investigating the ideas of all the great thinkers of the past. In particular, he studied the writings of a German philosopher named Hegel (1770–1831). Hegel claimed that historical progress was always the result of conflict between basic, widely held, opposing ideas – the old giving way to the new. But whereas Hegel believed that the Prussian state was history's final triumphant climax, Marx definitely thought otherwise .

Critical questions

Other young men around Marx were also stimulated and challenged by the writings of Hegel. They called themselves the "Young Hegelians," and met together as members of the "Doctors' Club" to discuss their philosophical ideas. Among them, Marx stood out as the most fiery, tempestuous personality of all. The breadth and depth of his learning seemed quite astonishing, considering that he was the youngest among them. For hours on end, sometimes deep into the night, amid piles of empty wine bottles and the aroma of countless cigars, they debated together. In particular, they criticized religion, denying the authority of Christianity and of Biblical texts. Marx believed that the Bible was nothing more than a series of fictional stories adapted to keep the ruling classes in power.

In Berlin, for the first time, Marx realized the appalling conditions in which the majority of people lived and worked, and the comparative luxury of the owning classes. After graduating as a Doctor of Philosophy in 1841, he began to write articles for a liberal newspaper called the *Rheinische Zeitung*. With little regard for the consequences, he fiercely attacked the policies of the Prussian government. When he became the editor shortly afterward, the newspaper's readership increased three-fold. Despite the activities of the government censors, who did their best to blank out its flood of criticism, Marx continued to write eloquently in support of the poor. Finally, however, it became clear that the paper would be closed down, and he resigned in disgust from his post as editor.

"In Germany there is nothing more I can do," he wrote to a friend. Before leaving the country for France, he and Jenny were married. Throughout the years to come, she would always be at his side.

Marx and the "Young Hegeliansm" would argue over philosophical points. It was here that he started to develop some of his most original ideas.

Words into weapons

Marx and his wife arrived in Paris toward the end of 1843. France was a country with strong revolutionary traditions, and the home of many of Europe's most radical thinkers and political activists. Like Marx, they wanted basic social changes that would favor the majority of people by doing away with all the oppressive practices of the past. But there were disagreements about how this should be done, and also about the exact nature of the society that would follow.

With one of his colleagues, Marx started a journal, attempting to blend the new German philosophical theories with the progressive, socialist politics of the French radicals. But there were only enough funds to produce one issue. By now, however, Marx was making contact with many people who thought as he did. Some, like Pierre-Joseph Proudhon (1809–65) and Mikhail Bakunin (1814–76), were well known, and had almost equal originality and influence as Marx. Others were ordinary workers whom he met and talked with in their clubs and cafés. Here, he felt, the "brotherhood of man" was a reality – not just an empty phrase.

He was continually reading and writing, "plunging into an endless ocean of books," as a friend put it. Marx meant to forge his philosophical theories into a weapon that the workers, or "proletariat" as he called them, could use to help overthrow the society that exploited and degraded them. Ultimately, he believed, there would be a classless society, with freedom and fullfilment for everyone. These were the ideas of

Mikhail Bakunin became a friend and eventually a rival of Marx.

communism. Marx had a tremendous grasp of facts, and knowledge of various social institutions. One area of knowledge would prove particularly important. This was economics, which concerned the production, distribution and consumption of goods. Then he met Friedrich Engels, and so began their lifelong, world-shaking friendship.

Marx hoped his newspaper would advance revolutionary change.

Comrades working together

It was an article written by Engels for his paper that had first convinced Marx of the need to study economics. Engels knew a great deal about the subject. His father owned cotton factories in both Germany and England, where he himself had lived for some time. But Engels was hardly typical of the owning classes, or "bourgeoisie" as Marx called them. He too was on the side of the proletariat, the people who actually produced the goods by their labor. On all the fundamental issues, the two men found themselves in complete agreement. And their partnership, as revolutionary thinkers and writers, and great personal friends, was to last for the rest of Marx's life.

Because of his journalistic work, which the Prussian government considered very threatening, Marx was expelled from France in 1845. For the next three years, he lived in Brussels, the capital of Belgium. His wife and baby daughter, also called Jenny, soon joined him, and shortly afterward, Engels arrived too. Here they started planning a number of books about the advance of history, and socialist thought in France, Germany and England. They also visited England for six weeks, where Engels was able to show Marx something of the widespread poverty and hardship that the spread of industry had created for the masses of workers.

By now they were involved with a number of revolutionary workers' organizations, one of which had groups in several European countries. Giving lectures, and building up a widespread network of contacts, Marx and Engels soon became the most effective members of what became known as the "Communist League." In 1847 the organization asked Marx and Engels to prepare a statement of its views.

The collaboration between Marx and Friedrich Engels was to last for nearly forty years. Both benefited immensely from their partnership as revolutionary thinkers.

"Workers unite!"

In February 1848, Marx and Engels produced a short book explaining all the main principles and aims of the League. It was called the *Communist Manifesto*. It portrayed social history as a series of "class struggles" between groups with varying economic power. In the

Workers living in great poverty began to unite to consider ways of changing their lot.

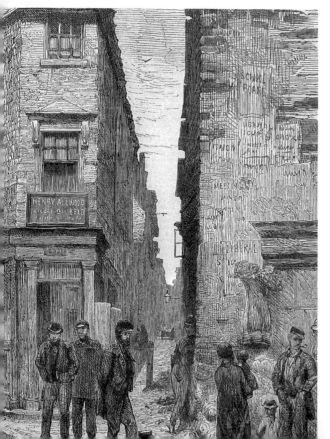

developing industrial world, it said, there were essentially just "two great hostile camps, two great classes directly facing each other – bourgeoisie and proletariat." The bourgeois "capitalist" system of wage-labor, and private profit for factory owners and employers, was "naked, shameless, direct, brutal exploitation," concentrating great wealth into the hands of a small minority.

But, the book went on, the system was also full of contradictions. The proletariat, becoming more and more aware of itself as a class, was poised to take over. Through violent revolution against its bourgeois oppressors, it would transform society totally. Private property would be abolished, and shared ownership of resources would "widen, enrich and promote the existence of the laborer." There would no longer be different classes opposing each other, only "an association in which the free development of each is the condition for the free development of all." The *Manifesto* concluded: "The proletarians have nothing to lose but their chains. They have a

Revolutionary groups met to discuss the ideas of communism.

nations, crowds were taking to the streets, demanding changes. Thrones tottered, kings and emperors trembled. Yet the *Manifesto* had not set things going; it was hardly known at the time. And these revolutions ended in failure. But throughout, Marx had his part to play.

world to win. Working men of all countries, unite!"

The *Communist Manifesto* was published in German, in an edition of 1,000 copies. Soon after, there was political upheaval all over Europe. In nearly all the continental

Workers fought in the streets in upheavals that shook Europe.

Revolutionary stirrings

Marx was preparing for an armed uprising in Belgium – buying weapons for the workers – when the *Manifesto* was published. He and Jenny were arrested by the Belgian police and expelled from the country. In France, where there had been a revolution, Marx was warmly welcomed by the new democratic government: "France, the free, opens her gates to you," he was told. He quickly made contact with exiles from Germany, beginning to plan tactics for the revolution that was starting there as well. With Engels, he prepared a list of Communist Party demands concerning Germany, and the following month they moved to the German city of Cologne.

Here Marx published a new newspaper called the *Neue Rheinische Zeitung*. Forcefully it argued the case for a "democratic-social red republic" in Germany. It supported all the revolutionary uprisings that were taking place elsewhere in Europe. There were many early victories, but

everywhere, the forces ranged against the workers were very strong. Marx's newspaper referred to the "pointless slaughters" carried out by those opposed to the revolutionaries, then stated, "There is only one way of shortening the murderous death pangs of the old society and the bloody birth pangs of the new society – namely, by revolutionary terrorism."

In February 1849, Marx was put on trial for "insulting public officials," and for calling for armed rebellion. He gave a lengthy speech to the jury and they found him "not guilty" – and thanked him for his informative lecture. Throughout the continent, however, the uprisings had been put down almost everywhere. Marx, who had been officially "stateless" since giving up his Prussian citizenship in 1845, faced expulsion again, from Germany. The final issue of the *Neue Rheinische Zeitung* was printed in red, a gesture of continuing revolutionary fervor. But for the time being, the cause was plainly lost.

Marx was expelled from Belgium for his revolutionary activities.

A life of poverty

Marx and his wife had two daughters and a son by this time, and a fourth child was expected soon. They were not allowed to settle in France, where they first went after leaving Germany, so as 1849 drew to a close, they arrived in London.

Long years of suffering and hardship lay ahead. For six years they lived in a small apartment in Soho, in conditions of acute poverty. Bills often had to be paid by leaving things at the pawnshop for a few pennies, and once they ate nothing but bread and potatoes for ten days. "I pity my wife," Marx wrote to Engels. "The main burden falls on her."

In the British Museum Marx could work undisturbed.

Engels was working as a representative for his father's business in Manchester. He earned about ten dollars a week, and always sent as much as he could spare. Without his help they could hardly have survived. Even so, two babies and their eight-year-old son, Edgar, died.

One visitor to the household was a spy for the Prussian police. He reported that the Marx family's two rooms were a jumble of shoddy, worthless items, and tattered, broken furniture covered in dust. "A rag-and-bone man would step back ashamed from such a remarkable collection," he wrote. He described Marx as "a man of genius and energy" – who rarely washed, and liked to get drunk. "He is often idle for days on end," the spy continued, "but when he has work to do, he works tirelessly, night and day." Marx spent much of his time working at a desk in the reading room of the British Museum. He had decided that conditions were not yet right for the Communist revolution.

The Marx family lived in a cramped, squalid apartment.

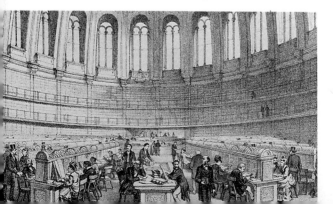

Better Days

In 1855 Marx wrote to Engels with some news: "A very happy event, the death of my wife's ninety-year-old uncle, became known to us yesterday. My wife gains £100, more if the old dog doesn't leave money to his housekeeper." A few months later, Jenny's mother also died, leaving a small legacy. The family were now able to move to a better house, in North London.

But the hard grind of poverty soon returned, and illness was a constant worry, with Jenny's health giving particular concern. Marx earned a little money with articles – some written by Engels – that he sent to the *New York Daily Tribune*. After the newspaper ended its connection with him, he tried to get a job as a clerk; but his handwriting was practically unreadable and his application was refused. In his economic studies, he was

Jenny suffered much ill-health, caused partly by their poverty.

Eleanor, Marx's youngest daughter, who was born in 1855.

continually reading and writing about money, yet he had virtually none in his pocket. Yet his daughter Eleanor, who grew up in North London remembered those years with affection. She recalled Marx sometimes "bubbling over with fun" when he played with his children, making up long, delightful fairy stories, and reading to them from books such as the *Arabian Nights*, and books of ancient legends.

In Germany, the workers' movement was growing again. Its leader, Ferdinand Lassalle, had great respect for Marx's ideas. They met several times, in Berlin and London. Marx respected Lassalle's ability to organize the workers, and hold crowds enthralled by his speeches. But he did not like or trust him. He thought Lassalle's revolutionary tactics were mistaken and was offended by his extravagant, comfortable lifestyle. Both men had their followers, and their rivalry threatened to become serious. But then, in 1864, Lassalle was killed in a duel. Despite their differences, this was a serious blow for Marx.

Ferdinand Lassalle, the leader of the German workers' movement, was Marx's rival for a brief time.

The "International"

Since his student days, Marx had never been close to his mother. When she died in 1863 it was the inheritance that mattered most to him. "In the circumstances," he wrote to Engels, "I am needed more than the old woman." Once again the family moved, to a house just around the corner, which was to be their last home. But visits to the pawnshop soon resumed, and Marx himself suffered from continual bouts of illness. The most painful and unpleasant were attacks of boils, which sometimes spread all over his body: "a truly proletarian disease," he called it.

In the mid-1860s, workers' organizations from many countries of Europe decided to group together to form a movement for radical change. This band, the "International Workingmens' Association," was composed of members of groups

holding differing opinons. They ranged from anarchists, who wanted to abolish the institution of "the state" altogether, to trade union leaders who believed progress could be made simply by putting pressure on the government. All agreed to unite, however, under a set of principles and rules prepared by Marx.

For several years, his work with the "International," as it

The First Congress of the First International, September 1866.

Marx was the dominant personality at the "International" meetings.

came to be known, was Marx's main preoccupation. He attended weekly meetings of its general council in London, and dealt with all of its important correspondence. He also wrote many of its pronouncements and reports on international problems, including the prospects of independence for Poland and Ireland, and on issues such as the length of the working-day, child-labor, and education. His views seemed quite moderate compared to those of his earlier years. But in 1867 he told Engels, "In the next revolution, which may be nearer than it seems, we – that is, you and I – will have this powerful engine in our hands." He was building for the future.

"Das Kapital"

The first part of Marx's great book on economics, *Das Kapital*, was published in 1867. Its subject was the capitalist "political economy" of the industrialized world. In close detail it examined how the capitalist system worked, analyzing the complicated relationships among labor, value, wages, prices and profits. It described the various ways in which the system exploited and harmed the workforce – the men, women and children living lives of wretched, hopeless poverty and endless toil – who produced the goods that made the ruling classes rich. But it also stated that the system was bound, someday, to collapse.

Marx spent half his life writing Das Kapital.

The Paris workers' "Commune" fought troops on the streets.

Crises in the world's "money markets" and economic depressions were signs of its underlying weakness. Sooner or later, the book claimed, "capitalism" would be replaced by communism: revolutionary changes were inevitable.

Das Kapital made no money for its author. Few people read it, and even fewer bought it. Nevertheless, within a few years, Marx's personal finances were considerably improved. Engels, who had inherited and then sold a partnership in his family's business, generously arranged to pay all Marx's outstanding debts, and allow the family an income of £350 per year. In 1870 Engels moved to London, where he became almost a member of the family himself.

Meanwhile, in the International, divisions had developed between the "Marxists," and those who believed in the anarchist doctrines of Mikhail Bakunin. The dispute worsened after some bloody events in France, in 1871. France had been defeated in a war against Prussia, but the workers of Paris refused to accept the situation. They set up a "Commune" in the city, declaring it to be a workers' state. For Marx, this was a necessary stage on the way to communism – the "dictatorship of the proletariat." But for the anarchists, any state, even one run by the workers, was necessarily oppressive.

The end – and the beginning

The violent excesses of the Paris Commune sent shivers up the spines of law-abiding citizens everywhere. However, it lasted only ten weeks, eventually being brutally suppressed by government troops. But during this time, Marx's name became more widely known. The *Communist Manifesto* was thought to be the Commune's main inspiration; and some people wondered if Marx himself had organized the uprising, from behind the scenes. The International then began to seem a menacing, dangerous association of violent fanatics. But in fact, it was rapidly breaking up. Bakunin's supporters were mounting a strong challenge to Marx's authority; and to avoid losing control, he voted to move its headquarters to New York. Effectively, this ended the International altogether.

During his last years, Marx continued to take an active

Eleanor would often accompany Marx to Karlsbad in his old age.

It was not until after Marx's death that his reputation as a great thinker really grew.

interest in the struggles of the workers, particularly those in Germany. He also continued to read extensively, and toward the end of his life began to take a serious interest in Russia. But he hardly hoped, any more, to see a successful revolution in his lifetime. And he could no longer work as he used to. Headaches, rheumatism and bronchitis continually plagued him, and with his daughter Eleanor he frequently took trips to the German spa town of Karlsbad, in search of a cure. His most carefree moments were when he played with his grandchildren, as he had once played with his daughters, in the his North London garden.

Jenny, his long-suffering wife, died of cancer in December 1881, and a year later, his daughter Jenny also died. Marx survived only another two months: it was as though his will to live had gone. Over the next twelve years, until his own death, Engels worked to finish *Das Kapital* from Marx's notes. He lived to see an enormous growth in Marx's reputation. But he never met Lenin or Trotsky, who led the Russian Revolution in 1917. Communism, in practice, belonged to the future.

Seventy years after his death, the Communist Party erected this gravestone in London, England to honor Karl Marx.

Important dates

Picture Credits

Glossary

Anarchist   Someone who condemns all forms of authority and advocates a social system based on voluntary cooperation.

Bourgeoisie   The "middle classes" in society; those who benefit most from capitalism.

Capitalism   A political-economic system, involving private ownership of goods and resources.

Communism   A political-economic system, involving shared ownership of goods and resources.

Democratic   A system of government based on the will of a majority of the people.

Economics   The study of the production and selling of goods for money

Liberal   Favoring political and religious freedom.

Marxist   A follower of the economic and political theories of Karl Marx and Friedrich Engels.

Paris Commune   A council of workers established in Paris in 1871, in opposition to the National Assembly. It was put down by government troops with much bloodshed.

Pawnshop   A place to which articles of value can be taken and left as security for a loan of money.

Philosophy   The study of ideas and beliefs, or systems of thought.

Political activist   Someone who believes in taking militant action to achieve a political end.

Progressive   Favoring political, economic or social advance.

Proletariat   The industrial "working class"; those who possess neither capital nor production means.

Prussia   The largest and most powerful of the independent states of nineteenth-century Germany.

Radical   Favoring fundamental changes in political, economic or social conditions.

Revolution   Wholesale political change: the overthrowing of one system in favor of another.

Romantic   A style in literature and art emphasizing individual emotions and the "inspiration" to be found in nature.

Socialist   Someone who favors economic and social equality among people.

Books to read

Marx and Marxism by Barbara Feinberg. Franklin Watts, 1985.

The Old Regime and the Revolution by Trevor Cairns, Lerner Publications, 1980.

Russia: A History of 1917 by Abraham Resnick. Children Press, 1983.

Russian Revolution and Its Aftermath by P. S. O'Connor. Heinemann Educational Books, 1969.

Unemployment by Jane Claypool. Franklin Watts, 1983.

The Worker in America by Jane Claypool. Franklin Watts, 1984.

Index